Influences

FLORAL DESIGN
IN NEW ZEALAND

Cheril Traill
1935 – 1994
The realisation of this book was one of her dreams.

PUBLISHED BY
Floral Art Society of New Zealand

Published by Floral Art Society of New Zealand Inc.
P.O. Box 19, Palmerston North, New Zealand.
Copyright © 1996 Floral Art Society of New Zealand Inc.
for text and Geoff Mason for photographs

First Published 1996
ISBN 0-473-03632-0

MANAGING EDITOR: Anne Mackay
PHOTOGRAPHIC COORDINATOR: Margaret Ashley
PHOTOGRAPHER: Geoff Mason
ART DIRECTOR: Donna Hoyle
BOOK DESIGN: Donna Hoyle Design
EDITOR: Alison Dench
AUTHOR OF TEXT: Anne Mackay
TYPESETTER: Fonts Typography
PRINTER: Everbest Printing Company

Printed in Hong Kong

Dedication

This book is published with pride to celebrate the thirtieth anniversary of the formation of the Floral Art Society of New Zealand, and to commemorate the culmination of the society's three-year tenure of management of the World Association of Flower Arrangers.

Influences is dedicated to the members of the Floral Art Society of New Zealand; to past members, who were wise and inspirational, and to present members, who find friendship and the joy of creative expression through the art of floral design.

Contents

Letter from the president of the World Association of Flower Arrangers

To celebrate their hosting of the World Association of Flower Arrangers Executive, the Floral Art Society of New Zealand decided to take the opportunity to publish a book of floral art. The WAFA New Zealand committee accepted responsibility for the content and production of this book.

Influences is a platform for New Zealanders to display their own unique style and the diverse range of plant materials available. I am sure this presentation will be very well received both internationally and in New Zealand.

Elaine C. Herbert.

Elaine Herbert

Letter from the president of the Floral Art Society of New Zealand

From the very beginning of time, our passage through life has been influenced not only by our own experiences but also by those of others. Despite cultural differences, we have a common bond that transcends all boundaries. It is a language that is simple and unique, yet so powerful that emotions and ideas can be communicated without uttering a word. I speak of flowers. Throughout the centuries and throughout the world, we have revered their uncomplicated perfection, exalting in nature's infinite combinations of colour, form and texture. It is through this appreciation that floral design has been developed and nurtured.

The society has great pleasure in presenting this book of floral creativity. The designers featured will take you on a journey of discovery, and while sharing their talents with the world they also introduce a wealth of flora from our beautiful country.

Momentous events and great achievements are certainly important, but quiet moments of contentment and small, unexpected delights also bring joy to our lives. As you work your way through this book, I hope you will take the time to contemplate and savour the marvels of nature.

Shirley Kittow

Introduction

When last century the early British colonists came to these shores to join the earlier Maori arrivals, they needed courage and an adventurous spirit to enable them to survive in a new world. Despite times of discord and dispute, the two cultures combined to establish a largely classless society where hard work seemed to be the only prerequisite for success. In the following years, many further waves of immigration from all over the world added to the richness of New Zealand's culture.

In a cosmopolitan society where the people value the environment more than most, where elitism is frowned upon and where a do-it-yourself attitude prevails, floral art has found its own niche. Unlike many of the allied arts, floral design is not expensive and is within reach of most. Many materials are there for the taking, in gardens, in the countryside or on the beach, ready to form the basis for creative expression. New Zealand floral designers will always draw inspiration from Europe, but they are beginning to appreciate more fully the challenges and freedom offered by a Pacific location. Like so many fields – fashion, interior design, the arts, gardening and architecture among them – floral art is now turning to the Pacific in the search for an indigenous style.

Members of the Floral Art Society of New Zealand prefer to be called floral artists or floral designers rather than flower arrangers because they feel these terms better reflect the art form to which they aspire. The word 'floral' is here taken in its widest botanical sense to include all plant forms: flowers, foliage, fruits, vegetables, barks, seaweeds, mosses, lichens, spathes, vines and roots.

The Floral Art Society of New Zealand Inc was formed in 1965 and has since grown to become a strong association of 4500 members within 125 clubs and fifteen areas. Over the years a succession of gifted society tutors, as well as visiting instructors, have shared their knowledge and special skills with members.

The society has established an education system and initiated courses and examinations. The very successful unit system of study for national floral art qualifications, introduced in 1983, has given judges, teachers and demonstrators the opportunity for quality education in the subject, and has increased the standard of work both nationally and internationally. The society has also put in place a certificate of practical design to acknowledge superior design skills.

In 1989 the society published *Flair*, its first reference book, and at the same time freed up some of the restrictions in competitive classes. These changes removed some of the uncertainties and put the emphasis on design rather than interpretation. As a result, members now strive for excellence in design above all else.

In 1981 the society became a founder member of the World Association of Flower Arrangers. In 1993 it assumed management for the 1993-96 WAFA term, culminating in the World Floral Art Show in Wellington, New Zealand, in April 1996. This milestone in the society's history, together with the precedent set by previous host countries, provided the incentive to produce a pictorial book celebrating the art of floral design in New Zealand.

Members of the Floral Art Society of New Zealand were invited to submit portfolios of their work, and from these the designers for the book were selected. The designers featured have chosen their own concepts and titles. The resulting record of floral design in New Zealand reflects the endless range of treasures with which Nature surrounds us and the endless creativity and ingenuity of the designers.

CHAPTER ONE
Environment

Beneath the Trees
Lorraine Ryan

*A basket made of palm fibre and vines is
filled with autumn fruits and foliage.*

Plant material: Malus 'Red Delicious', Pinus,
Sedum, Aesculus, Amanita muscaria,
Lycopodium, Parthenocissus tricuspidata,
Wisteria, Cornus capitata, Rosa 'Botany Bay'.

The two main islands of New Zealand are situated in the Roaring Forties of the South Pacific. The country enjoys a range of climates, all of which provide good conditions for growing plants; indeed, many introduced species grow better in New Zealand than in their country of origin. From the subtropical north to the temperate south, rainfall is plentiful most of the time. Both horticulture and floriculture industries are well developed, so that the variety of plant material available to buy is very wide, its quality is good and it is not expensive. Plant material arrives almost daily from markets around the world to add an exotic note.

New Zealanders live close to nature and tend to take the profusion of plants for granted. Urban areas have a multitude of parks and planted roadsides, and many commercial buildings are attractively landscaped. Almost every home in New Zealand, even in central city areas, boasts a garden of some sort. People in country areas live with an abundance of plant material around them, regardless of their fondness for gardens. Forests, bush, roadside, coastline, farm and mountain are within the reach of most people.

New Zealand has an exceptionally long coastline, and beaches yield a rich supply of material for the floral artist. High rainfall in many areas ensures there is an abundance of driftwood, as well as kelp, seaweeds, pumice stone and shells including paua (abalone). The great majority of the population live near to the coast; we are perhaps unconsciously influenced by the sea that surrounds us. Sand, wind and waves provide rhythms and patterns, while the timelessness and immensity of the ocean put man's endeavours into perspective and exert a pacifying influence.

Unique native plants give the landscape a distinctive character, but most New Zealanders take them for granted. It often takes a visiting floral artist to awaken an awareness of their many special features. Native forests have very few deciduous plants, but boast buttercups, lilies, liverworts, mosses and the largest tree ferns in the world; there are sheep-like plants, the world's smallest conifer, leafless plants and species with juvenile leaf forms, to name but a few unique characteristics.

Native plants are not highly coloured – a characteristic usually attributed to the fact that most are pollinated by the wind rather than by insects – but kowhai (*Sophora*), with its bright yellow flowers, and the red pohutukawa (*Metrosideros*) are exceptions. A lack of bright colour is, however, more than made up for by a rich tapestry of greens. Cascading *Dacrydium*, bold, shiny *Meryta sinclairii* and *Myosotidium* leaves, rough, fine textures of *Hebe* and *Podocarpus totara*, variegated *Pseudopanax*, *Griselinia* and *Phormium*, provide strong variation of textures and forms. Grey-leaved *Astelia* and *Senecio* are popular with floral artists, and other favourites include ladder ferns, ponga bark, weathered puriri wood *(Vitex lucens)*, shelf fungi and mosses. The forests abound with vines and their use gives strong movement to designs.

New Zealand designers use colour boldly and clearly. The pure, bright light in this part of the world favours the selection of strong hues.

As floral artists, we revel in the treasures the natural world has given us. Their influences are the cornerstone of our art.

Shifting Sands
Patricia Proctor

The rippling of sand is suggested by the horizontal placement of the driftwood. Perspex creates a mirage with the soft light of the poppies.

Plant material: Papaver nudicaule, sand-washed driftwood, Nymphaea lotus.
Other material: reef coral, smoky perspex.

Beauty of the Reef
Laurel Frogley

Sea life floats by within the safety of the reef.

Plant material: Anthurium, Phormium,
Protea cynaroides, kelp.

Clean and Green
Rhonda Hall

The clean, green lines are provided by the
horizontal strips of flax.

Plant material: Phormium, Cytisus,
Lycopodium, Dianthus, Rosa, Sophora.

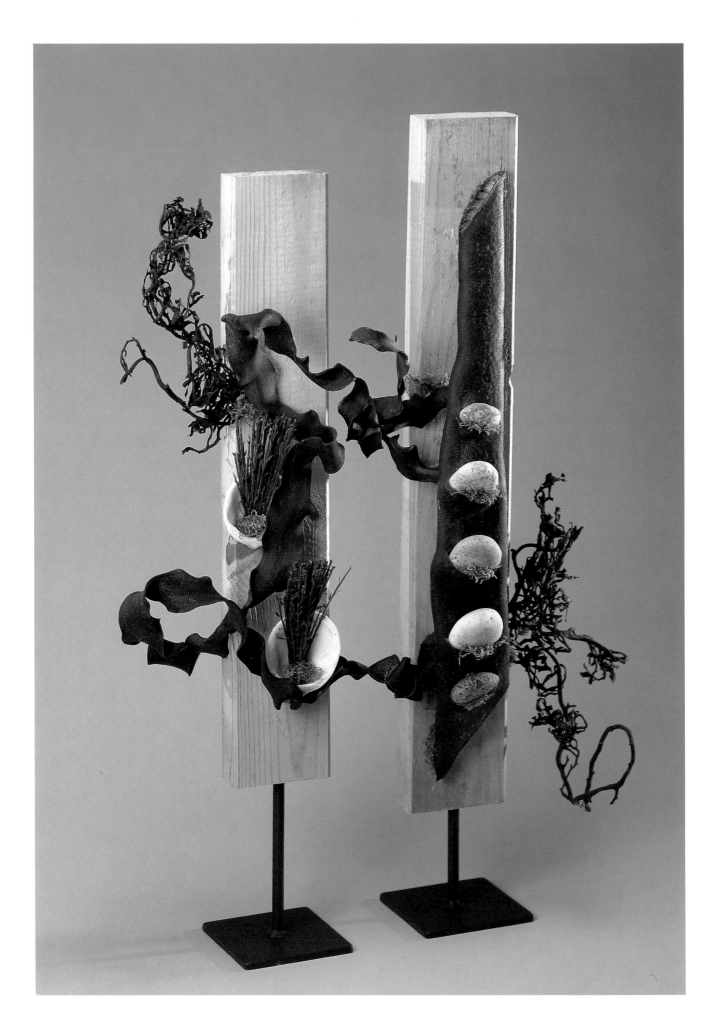

Sculptured by the Sea I
Pauleen Burfoot

A piece of driftwood swirls and surges like the sea that has sculptured it. The large roses are fashioned from astelia leaves.

Plant material: Astelia 'Silver Spear', Tecomanthe speciosa, driftwood.

High Tide
Rhonda Hall

Kelp, seaweed, shells and stones gathered on the southern coastline of New Zealand provide the materials. The stones have been pocketed in the kelp.

Plant material: Cytisus, kelp, seaweed, wood.
Other material: shells, stones.

Flight of Fancy

Lyn Amos

The sophistication of the design contrasts with the informality of the country gatherings.

Plant material: Asparagus asparagoides (Smilax), Muehlenbeckia, Phalaenopsis, Bambusa.

The Awakening
Ruth Orange

The unfurled centre spears of cabbage tree foliage form the flowers.

Plant material: Cordyline australis,
Phormium tenax, Myosotidium hortensia,
Polystichum, Pseudopanax crassifolium,
Solanum aviculare.

Cirrus
Margaret Ashley

A collection of flowers and budding branches casually arranged in matching pottery containers signals the approach of spring.

Plant material: Fraxinus excelsior, Iris, Ranunculus, Freesia, Leucadendron, Pelargonium tomentosum.

Fireball
Lorraine McMillan

*Texture, form and colour come together in a
strong, simple design mounted on puriri
wood.*

Plant material: Vitex lucens, Rosa
'Cappuccino', Astelia chathamica,
Muehlenbeckia.

Appliqué
Michelle Skelton

Zippers add an original touch to a tapestry of forms.

Plant material: Limonium, Gleditsia, Hydrangea macrophylla, Nothofagus solandri, mosses.
Other material: zippers, river stones.

Bush Walk
Anne James

The selection of New Zealand native materials was inspired by the designer's love of hiking.

Plant material: Phormium 'Tricolour', Nephrolepis cordifolia, Pittosporum, Pseudopanax 'Gold Splash', Lophomyrtus 'Katherine', lichened branches, fungi, weathered wood.

Oceania
Geraldine Bathurst

The rock oyster shells were found while walking along a North Island west coast beach.

Plant material: Limonium, Helleborus corsicus, Anemone, Eustoma grandiflorum.
Other material: rock oyster shells, fan coral.

Fire and Ice
Margaret Morriss

The stark outline of the wall hanging is balanced by contrasting lines.

Plant material: Betula pendula, Helichrysum, Astelia chathamica, Camellia, kelp, fungus.
Other material: horse mussel shells.

The Pearl
Elva Hegh

This work was inspired by the gift of the subtly coloured fungus.

Plant material: Vitis vinifera, Amaranthus, Coprosma propinqua var. latiuscula, Actinidia chinensis, fungus, Lycopersicon.

Coral Sea
Maureen van der Heyden

The swamp puriri wood, buried for centuries, was dug up and left to dry for two years before being blow-torched to remove the soft wood.

Plant material: Vitex lucens, Lilium.
Other material: fan coral.

Aspiration
Heather Hammond

*The colours and pattern of the pot are
repeated in the kauri wood and other
plant materials.*

Plant material: Cordyline indivisa, Banksia,
Lilium, Agathis australis, Butia capitata.

Light and Shadow
Elva Hegh

The small North Island town of Otaki, with the sea on one side and the forest on the other, is a wonderful growing area. The mix of materials tells the story.

Plant material: Phormium, Amaranthus, Chrysanthemum, Araujia, Pittosporum crassifolium, Asparagus 'Myersii', Carex, Meryta sinclarii 'Variegata', Zantedeschia, lichen, kelp.
Other material: paua shells.

Fruits of the Forest
Margaret Fox

Glowing karaka berries highlight an all New Zealand native design in a ponga (tree fern) ball.

Plant material: Corynocarpus laevigatus, Brachyglottis repanda, Pachystegia insignis, Agathis australis, Podocarpus dacrydioides.

Earthly Delights
Paula Wilson

*A gift of kauri bark from a Northland friend
combines with bundles of silver birch twigs
and root forms in a strongly textured design.*

Plant material: Agathis australis, Betula
pendula, Rosa, Magnolia grandiflora, root forms.

New Zealand is a nation of gardeners; surveys show that gardening is the most popular leisure activity. Garden visiting is becoming increasingly popular, and there is a growing appreciation of landscape values and design.

New Zealanders like to live outdoors as much as possible, and often entertain outdoors or go to the beach. The relaxed lifestyle and the climate make outdoor living and gardening possible all year round. Garden rooms, courtyards and patios – all complete with planters – are popular, and the division between the garden and indoors is becoming blurred.

It is little wonder, therefore, that many people wish to bring plants indoors, and to design with them to enhance their homes and workplaces, or for social functions and special occasions.

It is a feature of New Zealand floral design that artists very often make their own containers or work without obvious containers. New Zealanders have earned a reputation as do-it-yourselfers and innovators, and these traits are certainly part of the floral art scene. Mechanics and stands are continually being created and copied and give a versatility and freedom to designs that are not bound by the dimensions and style of a container.

New Zealand is a small country where most people have their own transport. In their travels within the country and overseas, floral artists are constantly soaking up new ideas and influences, which they adapt to their own needs.

In short, we are a casual, active and mobile nation. We enjoy the outdoors and wide open spaces of our sparsely populated, clean, green country, and we carry a passion for the environment indoors and into our floral art.

CHAPTER TWO
Lifestyle

Beacon
Margaret Wilkin

*Immersed in a brown study of a winter fire
and remembering the fires at sunset on a
Fijian island.*

Plant material: driftwood, Cordyline,
Rhipogonum scandens, Rosa 'Only Love',
Leucadendron 'Safari Sunset'.

Lazy Days of Summer
Laurel Frogley

A relaxed atmosphere is created by the puriri wood and the golden glow of sunflowers.

Plant material: Vitex lucens, Helianthus, Pelargonium, moss.
Other material: shells.

Corporate Lunch
Clem Cullen

A tempting display adds an original touch to lunch in the boardroom.

Plant material: Paphiopedilum, Anemone, Malus, Prunus, Solanum melongena, Citrus sinensis, Vitis vinifera.

Ice Maiden
Jennie Monro

Cool colours skate gracefully across the ice.

Plant material: Astelia, Iris, Protea, Fatsia
japonica.

Noble Vine
Elizabeth Konig

Gnarled grape vine makes a strong gesture.

Plant material: Magnolia 'Eleanor May',
Scindapsus, Phylica pubescens, Vitis vinifera.

Spanish Nights
Lorraine McMillan

The colours of the terracotta container inspired the choice of autumnal material.

Plant material: Restio tetraphyllus, Asparagus 'Myersii', Magnolia, Pelargonium, Nandina, Zinnia, Moluccella, Triticum, vine, bark.

Tumble into Autumn

Lorraine Ryan

The beautiful wooden container provided the starting point for a design featuring balls made from vine and root fibre.

Plant material: Phormium 'Yellow Wave', root fibre, vine, Chrysanthemum, Parthenocissus tricuspidata, Physalis alkekengi 'Franchetii'.

Tree's Company
Jenny Harris

*Prunings bound with leather combine with
natural materials to give a feeling of
nature's patterns of growth.*

Plant material: Amaranthus caudatus,
Zantedeschia, black fungus, Irish moss.
Other material: walnut burl.

Space Odyssey
Ngaire Clarke

Strong forms march into space.

Plant material: Protea cynaroides, Musa,
Xerophyllum.

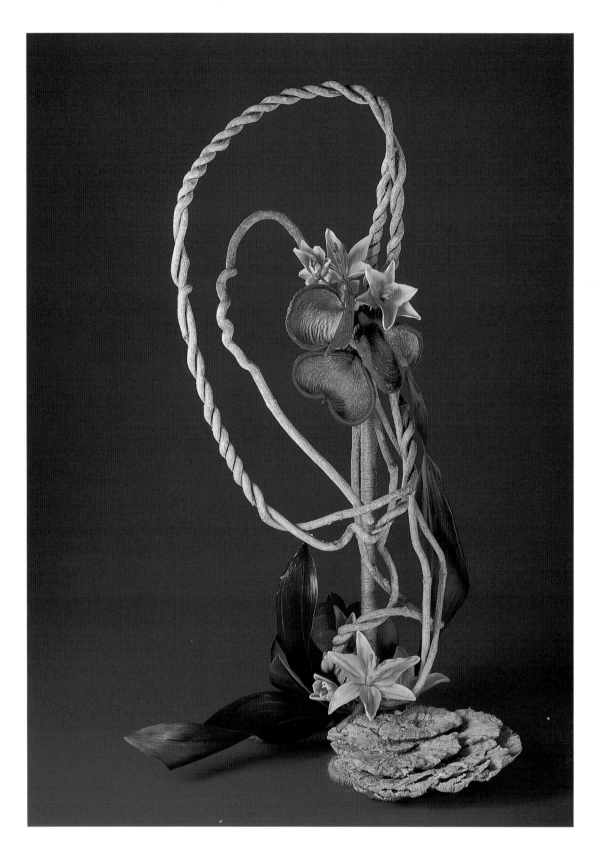

Lassoed
Laurel Frogley

Twisted vine provides strength.

Plant material: Araujia, Aspidistra, Magnolia,
Lilium, fungus.

Quicksilver
Colleen Fernie

Industrial materials inspire innovation.

Plant material: Anthurium, seed pods,
Cordyline.
Other material: metal mesh stand, mesh fabric.

Colour Break
Paula Wilson

Plant material, used with discipline, repeats the lines of the boxes.

Plant material: Phormium, Celosia cristata, Eucalyptus, Gerbera, Pinus, Beta, Citrus limon.

CHAPTER THREE

Heritage

Pacifika
Lois Morrow

*Cool colours and uncluttered forms offer a
taste of the Pacific Islands.*

Plant material: Rhopalostylis sapida, Astelia
solandri, Dysoxylum spectabile, Cordyline
australis.

In the 1850s, when large numbers of English and Scottish settlers first came to New Zealand, many of them had farming in mind. When the back-breaking toil of clearing the land and building a basic dwelling was done, the colonists planted gardens from precious seeds and carefully nurtured cuttings. For women isolated in a wild and lonely landscape, there was comfort in the familiar, and many planted flower gardens that reminded them of Home. Some also took an interest in indigenous flowering trees and shrubs and recorded the intriguing new species in fine watercolours.

For many in the towns life was easier and fortunes more easily come by. Traders and speculators installed extravagant formal gardens, complete with flower borders and statuary, but more often city dwellers planted informal cottage gardens that provided a ready supply of cut flowers.

Among the early European settlers, both rural and urban, skill with flowers was considered one of the accomplishments of a gentlewoman, and this attitude continued through to the post-war era. Wherever women gathered, for social events, at meetings or in the church, there was always someone whose turn it was to 'do the flowers'. At that time Constance Spry was one of the great influences on floral art.

In more recent times increased contact with Asia has brought about a marked change in the direction of this country's floral art. The influence of the visit in the early 1960s of Bernard Leach and Shoji Hamada is still seen in the work of potters; the emphasis changed in favour of minimalism, form, balance and line. The vessels they produced opened up a range of new possibilities for floral designers.

Although there is no evidence that floral art was a part of Maori culture, the weaving of flax (*Phormium*) and other native plants has always been an essential craft. Amongst the items produced are utilitarian kete (baskets), ropes and fish traps, through to highly decorative full-length flax fibre cloaks. The techniques employed in Maori weaving have often been used in the work of floral designers, some of whom break traditional boundaries and use flax in highly innovative ways.

The weaving, plaiting and printmaking of the people of the Pacific Islands is also emerging as a cultural influence. With the exception of the Cook Islands, where the bright, warm colours of tropical flowers are often used in tivaevae (quilts), the emphasis in Pacific Island crafts is on the strongly contrasting shades of brown, black and white. Shells, palm fronds and coral, symbols of the Pacific, are also frequently used as materials in New Zealand floral designs.

More recent immigrants, especially those from continental Europe and Asia, have helped to create an individual style for floral design in this country. This, coupled with the wonderful variety of plant materials available and a healthy growing climate, have made it possible for experimentation and exploration to flourish.

To Weave a Dream
Jill Marshall

Unity through diversity – the plant materials represent the mix of cultures in New Zealand.

Plant material: Phormium, Iris, Meryta sinclairii.

Lattice
Margaret Ashley

The ponga trunk was skeletonised by hand to reveal an intricate pattern.

Plant material: Cyathea medullaris, Rhipogonum scandens, Phalaenopsis, Aloecia.

Green Ice

Ngaire Clarke

*Material found growing on a cliff near the
designer's home blends elegantly with
materials from the garden.*

Plant material: Cortaderia jubata, Vincentia
sinclairii, Astelia nervosa, Rosa 'Athena',
Asparagus plumosus, Gypsophila.

Limelight
Elaine Herbert

Two ponga (tree fern) pots encouraged the choice of green and maroon materials.

Plant material: Cordyline australis, Leucadendron laureolum, Helleborus corsicus, Bergenia, Polystichum, Cyathea medullaris.

Biedermeier in Modern Manner
Heather Hammond

A modern biedermeier uses strong groupings of a variety of materials, while retaining the essential, compact spirit of the traditional style.

Plant material: Chrysanthemum, Alstroemeria, Asparagus myriocladus, Lunaria 'Variegata', Tulipa, Chiranthodendron pentadactylon, Ulmus, Cymbidium, Vitis, Banksia, Rosa, Berzelia, Dianthus, Equisetum.
Other material: cinnamae fabric.

Colourscape (OPPOSITE)
Margaret Morriss

Contrasts of colour and texture abound.

Plant material: Chrysanthemum, Araujia, Brassica, Platycerium bifurcatum, Erica, Rosa 'Delilah', Mahonia, Asparagus 'Myersii', Allium, Beschorneria yuccoides.

Asian Affair

Margaret Ashley

The Asian origin of many of these materials evoked this theme.

Plant material: Rhapis excelsa, long palm, Dianthus, Lilium, Actinida chinensis.

Sunburst

Anne James

The designer has a powerful love of colour,
particularly of pink and yellow together.

Plant material: Trachycarpus fortunei,
Phormium 'Dazzler', Chrysanthemum,
Protea ('Sylvan Pink' and 'Big Mink').
Other material: fabric, painted wire mesh.

Ethereal
Lois Morrow

Rising from the lake, an ancient puriri wood post supports the sacred waterlily of the Nile.

Plant material: Vitex lucens, Nymphaea caerula, Aloecia.

Pincushion
Helen Potter

The cherished textured pottery bowl came from the South Island's West Coast.

Plant material: Yucca filamentosa, Hedera, Melia azedarach, Asparagus 'Myersii', Luculia, Eustoma, Camellia, Asclepsia, Cupressus macrocarpa 'Aurea', Pieris, Backhousia citriodora.

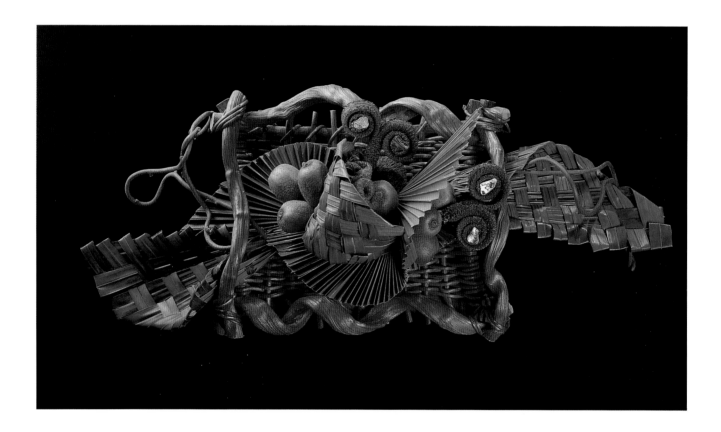

Pacific Rim
Maureen van der Heyden

A woven tray with natural curved vine combines with fruits and woven palm in a striking and very New Zealand design.

Plant material: Trachycarpus fortunei, Actinidia chinensis, curled pods.
Other material: paua shell.

Haere Mai
Colleen Fernie

Maori weaving created by a friend offers a Maori greeting.

Plant material: Rhopalostylus sapida, Phormium tenax, Cyphomandra, Washingtonia palm.

CHAPTER FOUR
The Arts

Aoraki – the Cloud Piercer
Margaret Wilkin

A favourite plant material is used in a design prompted by early childhood memories of the Mackenzie Country.

Plant material: Astelia chathamica 'Silver Spear', Anthurium.

Floral artists in New Zealand see themselves as part of the larger art world; after all, the fundamentals of design are common to all art forms. Inspiration is taken from many sources, and ideas are adapted to our own art form; painting, sculpture, photography, interior design, window dressing and the performing arts regularly give creative starting-points. New Zealanders have always been proficient at crafts, and pottery, glassware, embroidery and jewellery provide a wonderful well of ideas.

New Zealand floral artists have a love of floral theatre, which is a live performance of the art presented with the assistance of theatre facilities. This is also called 'demonstration', but the term 'floral theatre' portrays more accurately the entertainment value and theatrical skills involved, including lighting, drama, music, personal performance and spectacle. As in theatre itself, changes in style are always occurring, and there is an increasing subtlety of approach.

FASNZ is a founder member of the Arts Assembly of New Zealand, where it has always maintained a high profile. This has reinforced the society's wish to experience and participate fully in the arts scene. Financial assistance from Creative New Zealand, formerly the Arts Council of New Zealand, has greatly assisted the society in recent years as it strives for professionalism in administration.

The arts furnish us with enormous inspiration and understanding, with a meeting place of ideas and goals. Good art requires both originality and an appreciation of design excellence, and at times, challenges and tests boundaries of acceptance. Freedom of expression for the individual artist is essential, and the society aims to provide encouragement for those who seek new paths, while ensuring that our art still expresses beauty and gives pleasure.

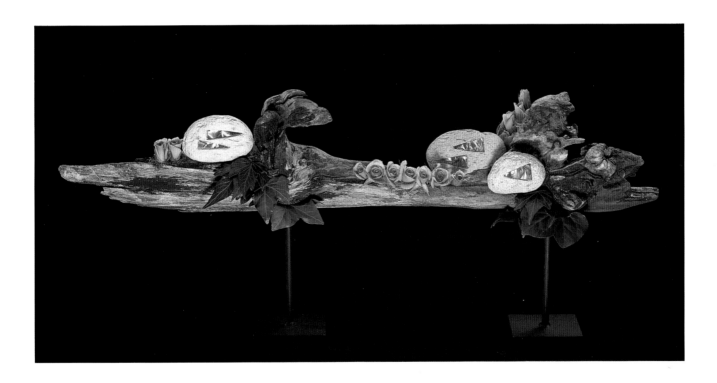

Inlaid and Overlaid
Rhonda Hall

The driftwood was the starting point and the allied arts inspired a design which includes pumice stone inlaid with copper to complement the roses.

Plant material: Hedera, Rosa 'Loving Touch', driftwood.
Other material: pumice stone, copper sheeting.

Predator
Colleen Fernie

A design based on the discovery of a piece of wood, found on a farm while returning from a floral art journey.

Plant material: Magnolia grandiflora, Chrysanthemum, Kalanchoe beharensis, Garrya elliptica, weathered wood, reeds.

Forest Guardian
Anne Mackay

The majesty of a pine forest provided the inspiration for a pine needle sculpture. A whimsically placed kiwifruit vine provides the final signature.

Plant material: Pinus, Actinidia chinensis, Hedera, moss.

Palmistry
Gloria Margison

Inspiration was found in the shapes of the palm spathes.

Plant material: Washingtonia robusta, Phalaenopsis.

Sculptured by the Sea II
Pauleen Burfoot

A dramatic composition of shapes carved by the sea.

Plant material: Butia capitata, Zantedeschia, mushrooms, Aesculus, Eleocharis sphacelata.

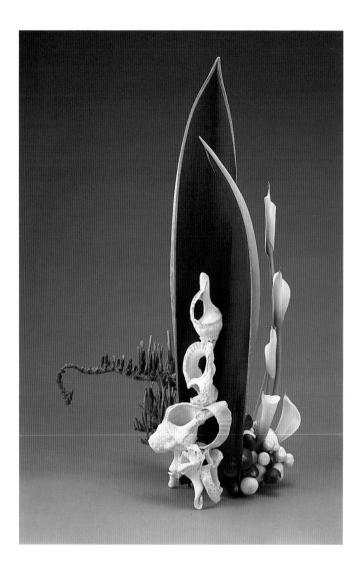

Kinetics
Michelle Skelton

This design was inspired by the work of artist Bridget Riley.

Plant material: Chrysanthemum, kelp.
Other material: painted wood.

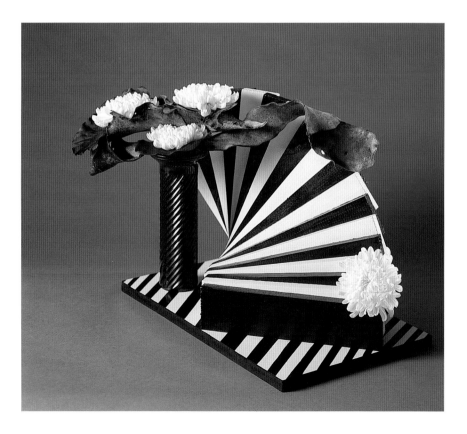

Anglepoise
Gloria Margison

The use of bold colour and angles achieves a modern focus.

Plant material: Anthurium, Aspidistra, Muehlenbeckia, Strelitzia reginae.

The Midas Touch
Geraldine Bathurst

The acacia bark was already in the wonderful sculptural shapes when found, and the lurex fabric only serves to enhance the form.

Plant material: Acacia, Trachycarpus fortunei, Billbergia, Camellia.
Other material: lurex fabric.

Aotearoa New Zealand
Jill Marshall

The copper plaque represents the sun, which each day rises first over New Zealand, and the driftwood symbolises the land of the long white cloud, wrapped in greenery and shrouded in white.

Plant material: Rhapis excelsa, Eustoma grandiflorum, Lilium 'Marco Polo', weathered wood.

Interwoven
Maureen van der Heyden

An intriguing pottery container is mirrored in the pattern of the woven cane.

Plant material: Aloecia, Protea, Actinidia chinensis, cane.

Rustic Reverie
Moira Moore

A collection of containers and a special twist of vine set off the cheery sunflowers.

Plant material: Helianthus, Viburnum odoratissimum.

Encirclement
Elva Hegh

The windblown flax flower stem suggested to the designer the use of the spherical pot.

Plant material: Phormium cookianum, Carex, Garrya elliptica, Anthurium.

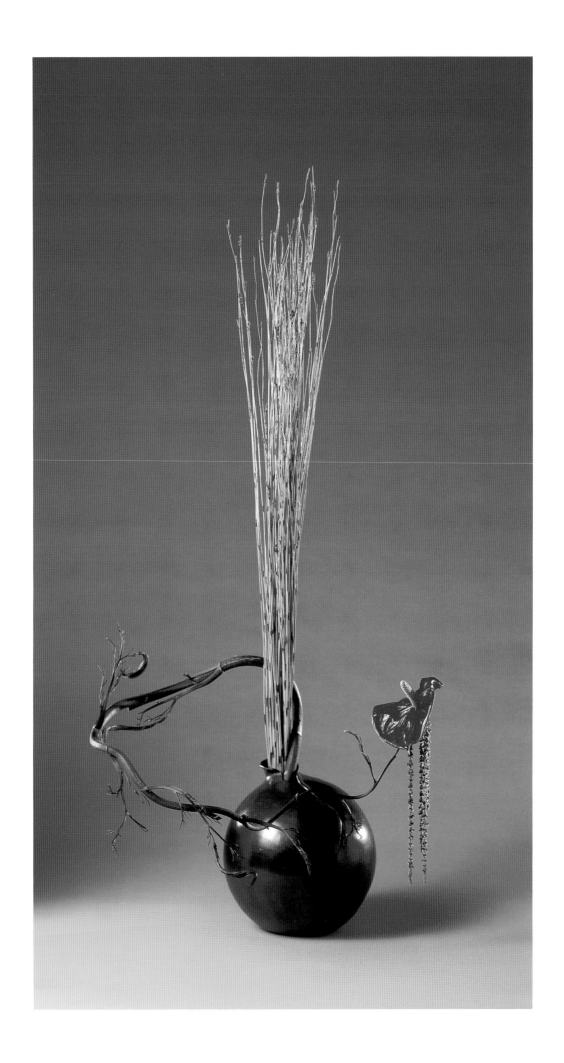

Rose Rhapsody

Moira Moore

Palm spathes provide the striking sculptural features for a design arranged in a slab container.

Plant material: Phoenix canariensis, Rosa 'Lady Rose', Limonium latifolium.

Sunshower
Margaret Fox

Lapageria blooms are featured with stunning simplicity.

Plant material: Lapageria, Philodendron rubrum, Echeveria.

Migration
Margaret Wilkin

A beautiful pot by Bronte of Motueka provided both the inspiration and the challenge.

Plant material: Strelitzia reginae, Anthurium.

Desert Walker
Elizabeth Konig

Tortured willow provides the form of the desert walker.

Plant material: Salix matsudana 'Tortuosa', Xerophyllum, Scindapsus 'Marble Queen'.
Other material: rope.

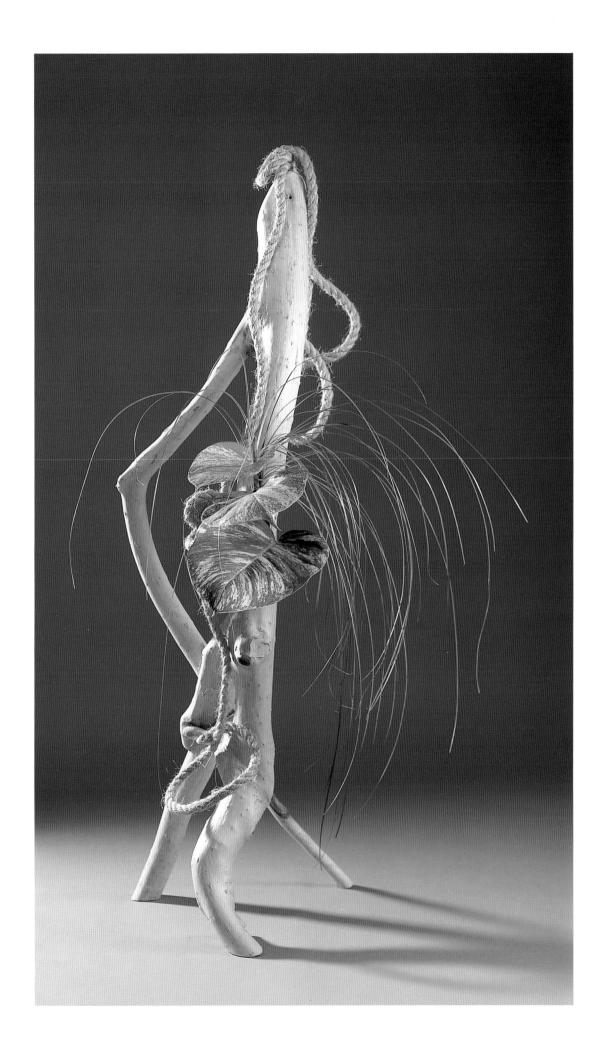

Out of the Depths

Eleanor Jones

*The wood, which is hundreds of years old,
needed minimal decoration.*

Plant material: Vitex lucens, Phormium
'Yellow Wave', Scleranthus uniflorus.

Raku
Jenny Harris

The colours of the ceramic pot provided the inspiration.

Plant material: Nothofagus solandri,
Parthenocissus tricuspidata, Zantedeschia.

Thorns and Roses
Anne Mackay

Spheres of rose prunings were formed over balls of snow. After the snow melted, they were enhanced with the addition of gilding and fresh roses.

Plant material: Rosa 'Cappuccino'.

Coir, Copper and Couture
Patricia Proctor

The designer's fascination with media and with couture styling comes through clearly in this work, with its focus on weaving and a crustaceous use of nature's textures.

Plant material: kelp, Discaria toumatou, Paphiopedilum, Cyphomandra, Gerbera, Rosa, Chrysanthemum, coconut fibre, dates, shallots, walnuts, lichen.
Other material: copper wire, mesh, strapping.

CHAPTER FIVE
Celebrations

Pearl Anniversary
Lorraine McMillan

A delicate design staged on a perspex and glass stand.

Plant material: Limonium 'Emille', Senecio maritima, Delphinium belladonna, Rosa, Tulipa.
Other material: nautilus shells.

All around the world flowers play an important role in festivals and celebrations, whether in the traditional carpet of flowers at Genzano, Italy, on the feast of Corpus Christi, the Tournament of Roses parade at Pasadena, California, on New Year's Day, or the Blossom Festival in the orchard town of Alexandra, New Zealand. In this country flowers feature strongly at weddings and funerals, as well as at parties and celebrations. On a more informal level, the New Zealand home entertainer will often have flowers on the buffet or dining table.

As elsewhere in the world, church weddings often feature large traditional designs; floral artists particularly enjoy creating displays for churches, relishing the opportunity to relate designs to architecture and backgrounds not encountered in other settings. The bride and her attendants almost always carry flowers, and many also wear them in their hair. Likewise, the groom and his attendants usually wear a single flower on the lapel. Outdoor weddings, which are very popular, include flowers on a table or a stand, or in an arch. Floral designs for wedding receptions show great variety; while many favour the traditional table posies, often including candles, others prefer more modern or novel themes.

Floral tributes feature less and less at funerals as many families ask mourners not to give flowers; in this case a large casket spray will be the central floral feature. Fresh flowers are available not only at florist shops but also at many local grocery stores, and bouquets are often given on special occasions, for illness, sympathy or friendship, or simply as a courtesy gift to a host. Traditional wrappings of cellophane and green florists' paper are giving way to brightly coloured paper and tissue, and brown paper or hessian tied with raffia.

In New Zealand Christmas falls in midsummer. The traditional colours of red, white and green still feature, but in a different way. Red-flowering pohutukawa, sometimes called the New Zealand Christmas tree, are part of the North Island Christmas landscape. Roses and lilies are firm favourites, while holly and ivy give a reminder of our European heritage. Many families have a Christmas tree of pine or douglas fir, but this creates another antipodean Christmas challenge: the soft, new foliage tends to wilt in the summer heat. Wreaths and topiary trees of dried materials combine happily with fresh summer flowers to celebrate Christmas in this part of the world.

Many floral artists find full or part-time employment providing designs for special occasions, as well as for the hospitality industry and the corporate sector. In recent years there has been an increasing tendency for corporate decor to feature floral art; the style of design has to fit in with the tempo of modern business, and is often sleek, smart and strong in colour.

For New Zealand floral designers, celebrations provide a catalyst for the full expression of their creativity. While they may be inspired and influenced by history, culture, art and the environment, they still seek to interpret the art form in a way that is entirely their own. It is a goal already achieved by those whose work is displayed in this book. May floral art flourish in the future and continue to give joy and creative expression to those who seek its rewards.

Winter Wedding
Anne James

Special flowers for a happy occasion.

Plant material: Thryptomene, Jasminum, Asparagus plumosus, Lunaria, Aspidistra, Chrysanthemum, Camellia, Luculia.

Pink Profusion
Lyn Amos

A classic style celebrates the designer's love of flowers.

Plant material: Lilium 'Joy', Rosa 'Porcelaine', Delphinium consolida, Jasminum, Antirrhinum, Michaelia figo, Nephrolepis cordifolia.

The Glory of the Garden
Anne Mackay

A celebration of flowers, fruit and vegetables.

Plant material: Eustoma grandiflorum,
Chrysanthemum, Phylica pubescens, Lilium,
Vitis vinifera, Prunus, Brassica, Citrus lemon,
Cryptomeria japonica 'Cristata', Petroselinum
crispum.

Softly Haloed

Lyn Amos

The Easter theme is portrayed in an innovative manner.

Plant material: Asparagus plumosus, Chrysanthemum, Phormium, Rosa, Lilium, Meryta sinclairii, Brassica oleracea 'Gemmifera', Hedera, Capsicum.

Mystique Glow
Heather Rizzi

Candles and flowers provide a warm welcome.

Plant material: Bambusa, Alstroemeria, Leucadendron 'Fire Glow', Achillea, Hydrangea, Fatsia japonica, Asparagus 'Myersii', Hedera canariensis 'Glorie de Marengo', Adiantum, Rosa 'Sonia', Asparagus plumosus.

Harvest Gatherings

Muriel De Stefano

A festival garland.

Plant material: Cape gooseberries, Malus, Citrus limon, Allium, Helichrysum argyrophyllum, Helichrysum bracteatum, Anaphalis margaritacea, Hedera, Fagus sylvatica purpurea, Lycopodium, mixed berries, cones and nuts.

Hallowe'en

Paula Wilson

Pumpkins hold the centre of the design, nature provides the exciting forms.

Plant material: Cucurbita, Betula pendula, Gerbera, Vitis vinifera, Castanea sativa.

Moonlight
Geraldine Bathurst

Two perspex stalagmites add a distinctive touch to an understated design.

Plant material: Rosa, Aloecia.
Other material: crystallised branches, perspex.

An Age of Romance
Margaret Morriss

A moss covered column lends an elegant air.

Plant material: Prunus, Garrya elliptica, Rhododendron 'Christmas Cheer', Camellia 'Laurie Bray', Cymbidium, Asparagus plumosus.

It's Christmas Time

Helen Potter

A modern interpretation of a Christmas wreath.

Plant material: Aspidistra, Ilex, Hedera,
Actinidia chinensis, Passiflora, cones.
Other material: glass beads, copper wire,
ribbon, Austrian birds, lacquered cherries,
baubles.

Hearth and Home

Elaine Herbert

Terracotta and fabric complement the textures of vegetables and other plant materials.

Plant material: Magnolia grandiflora, Musa, Italian parsley, Triticum, Asparagus, scaloppini, Citrus, fungus.

Yuletide
Muriel De Stefano

A rich festive gathering of natural materials combined with a touch of glamour.

Plant material: Ilex, Buxus, Hedera, Papaver, cones, berries, nuts, Malus, peach stones.
Other material: Christmas silk baubles, beads.

Designers

Lyn Amos (Auckland). Lyn believes that flowers are an integral part of our inner being. Her involvement with flowers has enriched her life, broadened horizons and given a deeper perception of the infinite beauty in the magical floral world. International contacts have expanded the philosophy that flowers bridge all barriers.

Margaret Ashley (Auckland). Margaret appreciates nature's artistry in the materials she gathers, such as branches, bark and wood, and prefers to use them naturally and without manipulation. She loves to work with flowers and colour, and gains great inspiration from the books in her extensive collection.

Geraldine Bathurst (Auckland). Originally from a South Island farming background, Geraldine made a career in the fashion industry and now lives in Auckland. Gardening, sailing, extensive travel and a fascination with flowers from a very early age all influence her artistic ideas.

Pauleen Burfoot (Auckland). Pauleen has lived in both rural and urban areas, but always near the sea. She is a fine arts graduate with a flair for colour and innovative design.

Ngaire Clarke (Whangaparaoa). The versatility of both native and exotic foliages, which have always been readily available, are a constant source of inspiration for Ngaire and feature strongly in her designs. She particularly enjoys exploring modern European styles.

Clem Cullen (New Plymouth). Clem's life has been spent in a busy rural community. She developed a love of all growing things at an early age, influenced by her father who was a keen gardener and rose grower. She has been very involved with floral art for many years.

Muriel De Stefano (Wellington). Muriel is a founder member and now life member of the Floral Art Society of New Zealand. She has a special talent for miniature designs and wreaths. Besides floral art, she also loves horticulture and allied arts.

Colleen Fernie (Auckland). Inspiration for Colleen's creative designs comes from a variety of sources, including allied arts. She enjoys using strong, bold forms and creating new dimensions, often with the aid of a glue gun. Teaching others provides a special joy.

Margaret Fox (Wellington). Margaret has a lifetime association with flowers. Her family were nurserymen and florists, and visits to flower shows have taken her all around New Zealand and the world. In her retirement she is surrounded by 800 pot plants.

Laurel Frogley (Auckland). Laurel has always lived in a city environment, which has provided endless inspiration for her designs. She has particularly enjoyed extending her knowledge through the educational opportunities available from the Floral Art Society of New Zealand.

Rhonda Hall (Winton). From an early age Rhonda's senses were captured by plant material, seaside gatherings and art. She likes to have convincing line and form in her work, enjoys mystery and expects a strong visual message to be conveyed.

Heather Hammond (Waikato). Heather was encouraged to arrange flowers from an early age by her mother. She has lived in rural areas all her life and takes pleasure from using indigenous plant materials. She enjoys the challenge of designing in many different styles and incorporating a diverse range of materials.

Jenny Harris (Christchurch). Jenny is fortunate to have experienced both city and country living and feels this has given her an insight into both lifestyles; each has an influence on her designing. Working closely with flowers and playing with nature has brought a sense of awareness and harmony to her life.

Elva Hegh (Otaki). Shaping and adjusting space in design has always held tremendous appeal for Elva, and determined the direction of her work. An early interest in abstract design endures, despite the many other styles she has explored over thirty-five years of involvement.

Elaine Herbert (West Otago). Elaine has always lived in the country and enjoys the natural environment and materials readily available. Her maternal grandmother, who was an avid gardener, designer and artist, proved inspiration for her creative expression.

Anne James (Feilding). Views of rolling hills and mountains from her windows and the colours and textures of her garden are constant sources of pleasure and inspiration for Anne. Tramping in national parks and on local walkways provide a special joy.

Eleanor Jones (Auckland). After spending years within the disciplines of architecture, where the results are likely to be in the environment for a long period of time, Eleanor has found it a delight to design with more ephemeral materials. She loves the freedom of working with the colours and forms provided by nature.

Elizabeth Konig (Auckland). Elizabeth was first introduced to the world of floral art on an overseas posting in Kenya. On returning home, she found the wealth of lush plant material growing in Auckland's subtropical climate inspired her to learn more about this challenging art form.

Anne Mackay (Otago). Anne lives on a high-country farm surrounded by a large garden, rolling hills, billowing tussock and trees. She enjoys the challenge of using simple, natural materials in unexpected ways in contemporary design.

Lorraine McMillan (Wellington). Lorraine has lived in many parts of New Zealand. The varying plant materials, diverse scenery and strong contrasts in weather patterns, as well as the many exhibitions of art and craft she has viewed, have all inspired her creativity.

Gloria Margison (Auckland). Gloria enjoys the relaxed lifestyle of Auckland. She works with natural materials and seeks inspiration from the forms she finds on beaches and in the bush. Bold statements and modern colours influence her work, which can be futuristic, classical, European or Oriental in style.

Jill Marshall (West Otago). For Jill, floral art is an emotional response to nature. She enjoys the challenge of working with living plant material to create ideas inspired by the land and the varied seasons of the farming area in which she lives.

Jennie Monro (Palmerston North). Jennie's many interests include handcrafts, bush walking and watercolour painting, all of which provide inspiration for her designs. During her term as national president in 1981 Jennie attended the inaugural meeting of WAFA in London.

Moira Moore (Auckland). Since childhood Moira has been influenced by the arts. Besides floral art, she has also studied Ikebana, which has helped her to master the use of fewer materials and sculptural form. She also teaches the piano.

Margaret Morriss (Palmerston North). For Margaret, inspirations abound in the natural world, in music, dance and culture. Design begins with an idea, followed by innovation, experimentation and, finally, the joy of achievement and the thrill of creative expression.

Lois Morrow (Auckland). Lois has always had a love of fauna, flora and floral design. She believes in the need for communication and awareness through expression of beauty and harmony, and very successfully combines and exhibits floral design and photography.

Ruth Orange (South Canterbury). Ruth lives on a deer farm and finds her floral inspirations are influenced by her rural outlook, her large garden and the nearby mountains in a very picturesque part of New Zealand.

Helen Potter (Waikanae). Helen has a background in both home science and horticultural ventures, and is a keen golfer. She devotes a large part of her time to floral art and particularly enjoys designing work for photography.

Patricia Procter (Christchurch). For Patricia, floral designing is like a long garden path with no end, each turn providing new inspirations and challenges. Flowers have always been part of her life, and her first understanding of design came from the landscape of northern Southland, where she once lived. She has a great interest in the allied arts.

Heather Rizzi (Winton). With a rural background and a career in nursing, Heather has a great love of nature. She enjoys china painting as well as floral art, and likes to share these artistic talents with everyone.

Lorraine Ryan (Tokoroa). A childhood on a central North Island farm surrounded by a large garden led to Lorraine's life-long interest in flowers. She gardens extensively, and finds floral art fulfils a creative urge, inspired by the treasures nature provides.

Michelle Skelton (Auckland). Michelle was brought up in Northland and now lives in Auckland. She has a background in business management. The arts have greatly influenced her designing, particularly the work of Bridget Riley, Wassily Kandinsky and James Gleick.

Maureen Van Der Heyden (Thames Valley). For Maureen, inspiration comes from nature, and she finds bush walks, driftwood and unusual plant materials often spark new concepts. Her interest in a wide variety of crafts has added interesting techniques to her floral art. She enjoys sharing her skills and knowledge with others.

Margaret Wilkin (Auckland). Because she is a gardener, the challenge to create beautiful designs to do justice to the plant material she loves is Margaret's life's work and pleasure. This is the challenge that propels her to learn all she can, to find newer and more innovative ways of designing with plant material and to compete with the best in the world

Paula Wilson (Winton). Paula lives in rural Southland and before floral art took over her life, her interests were speech and music. She has a profound love of flowers and the world of nature, and is continually looking for design potential in natural materials.